Shaping Your World Through Prayer

Kennetha J. Moore

MIKE MOORE
MINISTRIES

Shaping Your World Through Prayer
Copyright © 2022 by Kennetha J. Moore
Paperback ISBN: 978-1-7369777-8-1

Published in the United States by
Mike Moore Ministries, Inc.
www.mikemoore.com

Printed in the United States of America
All rights reserved. No part of this book may be reproduced, stored in a retrieval system, or transmitted in any form or by any means with-out expressed written permission of the author. Any internet addresses (websites, blogs, etc.) in this book are offered as a resource. They are not intended in any way to be or imply an endorsement by Mike Moore Ministries, nor does Mike Moore Ministries vouch for the content of these sites for the life of this book.

Unless otherwise indicated, all Scripture quotations are taken from the KING JAMES VERSION (KJV): KING JAMES VERSION, public domain.

Scriptures marked NKJV are taken from the NEW KING JAMES VERSION (NKJV): Scripture taken from the NEW KING JAMES VERSION®. Copyright© 1982 by Thomas Nelson, Inc. Used by permission. All rights reserved.

Scriptures marked NIV are taken from the NEW INTERNATIONAL VERSION (NIV): Scripture taken from THE HOLY BIBLE, NEW INTERNATIONAL VERSION®. Copyright© 1973, 1978, 1984, 2011 by Biblica, Inc.™. Used by permission of Zondervan

Scriptures marked NAS are taken from the NEW AMERICAN STANDARD (NAS): Scripture taken from the NEW AMERICAN STANDARD BIBLE®, copyright© 1960, 1962, 1963, 1968, 1971, 1972, 1973, 1975, 1977, 1995 by The Lockman Foundation. Used by permission.

TABLE OF CONTENTS

Introduction 5
    Scriptures on the Power of Words 9
Preface 13
In Christ Realities 15
Prayers for:
    Pastor 19
    Leaders 23
    Local Leadership 29
    Body of Christ 33
    The Lost 37
    Armed Forces and Military Personnel 41
    Individual Members of Your Church 45
    Nation 51
    Salvation 55
    Spiritual Growth 61
    Believing for a Mate 65
    Marriage 69
    Family 75
    Pregnancy 81
    Children 85
    Youth 91
    Challenge in the Conception of a Child 97

Decision-Making 103
Wisdom 107
Prosperity.. 111
Christian Business Owner 117
Career 123
Healing 127
First Holiday Without a Loved One......................... 133
Protection 137
Fear... 141
Favor... 145
Low Self-Esteem 149
Positive Affirmations 153
Journaling pages 155
About the Author 161
About Mike Moore Ministries.. 162

Introduction

Proverbs 18:21 says, "Death & Life are in the power of the tongue: and they that love it shall eat the fruit thereof."

Our world is framed by words. The words God spoke out of His mouth have created everything. Yet, the Bible says in the first chapter of Genesis that the earth was without form, void, and dark. So, how can God have what He wanted when the earth was without? "**And God said**, Let there be light: and there was light" (Genesis 1:3). God created the world and what He wanted by the words of His mouth. In other words, what we experience in life is the result of the words we consistently say about ourselves.

The words we speak regularly are producing the things (fruits) we are experiencing. Genesis 1, verses 9, 11, 14, 20, 24, 26, 29, and 31 says God saw what He created with the words spoken out of His mouth, and it was very good. Speaking faith-filled words are how God created things in this world. If we are born again Christians, then God is our Father, and we should imitate and follow His pattern of creating by using the words of our mouths.

We should confess the Word consistently, which is to agree with or say the same thing that God says about us or about our circumstances. This is His system of creating life; therefore, we should learn what He has to say about it and benefit from His way of creating things. Few Christians recognize the connection between their personal success in life and the words of their mouths. There are numerous Scriptures in the Bible where God shows us the connection between the words that we speak over ourselves, our circumstances, and our outcome in life.

One of my favorite Scriptures that I try to keep before my conscience is Proverbs 18:21 which says: "Death and life are in the <u>power of the tongue</u>: and they that love it shall eat the fruit thereof." This Scripture is saying that we can create death or life (a blessing or a curse, good or evil, success or failure) just by the words that we consistently say over our lives. Our words affect our thoughts. If our words are negative, our thoughts will be negative. If our thoughts are positive, our words will be positive. We can create our world just by what we speak over ourselves. Notice that it says the tongue has power. One definition of the word "power" is: The capacity or ability to direct or influence the course of events in life. The words we consistently speak over our lives have the capacity to influence the course of events in our lives. Notice it says that we shall have the fruit that we <u>consistently</u> say over our lives (and in our world). Every word we speak contains life or death. Every day we are speaking death or life to our lives.

Years ago, I lived in Hueytown, Alabama. One morning, I volunteered to read to a class of elementary school kids. After returning home, I noticed some young men leaving the house next door. When I went into my house, I realized that they had broken in and stolen several items in my home. I immediately called the police. When the officers came to my house and wrote a report of the burglary, one police officer said that I probably would not get my stolen items back. Once I heard his report, I went into the bathroom and reminded God that I was a tither and gave offerings. His Word said that He would

Introduction

rebuke the devourer for my sake (see Malachi 3:10-11). I had been taught several lessons by Pastor Michael D. Moore on the importance of the words we speak over our lives. I understood the power of my words, and it was important what I said from that exact moment. I said to myself, "I will get my items back and more."

About 4 hours later, the police called and said they caught the thieves at a pawn shop, and most of my items would be returned. Michael K., my son, about 9 years old then, came crying to me because they had stolen his Grant Hill jersey, and he had believed God for the jersey. I immediately told him to watch what he said from that point on, and I told him to say, "I will get my jersey back." Later that night, the police called to ask if we had a basketball jersey stolen, and I said yes. We went to the police station to pick it up.

I also had a birthstone ring that my sister had given me in the 4th grade. I didn't get that back, and I was not satisfied. I told God I didn't know how He was going to do it, but I wanted my ring back or a better ring. Later, a friend of mine shared my story with one of her friends in New Mexico. This lady owned a jewelry store, and she was led by God to bless me with a birthstone ring and other jewelry. The ring that she gave me had diamonds around it and my other ring did not.

God did exceedingly abundantly above all that I could ask or think because I watched what I was saying over my circumstances. I framed my world by the words of my mouth. I didn't say we will never get our stuff back. I said what I desired, and my desire was to get my stuff back because I am a tither. What are you saying consistently over yourself and your situation? Are you saying:

- I am healed and whole, or I am sick all the time? I will never get over this condition.
- I don't have any money, or God supplies my needs according to His riches in glory.
- I will never be able to buy a house, or I live in a goodly house filled with good things.
- I can't afford this, or God supplies my needs, and the favor of God is on my life.
- "God never talks to me?" Is that what you want? No, you don't! You should say, "I clearly hear God when He talks to me."
- "I can't understand the Bible," or "I get revelation knowledge and direction from God's Word."

Watch what you are saying over your life. If you want blessings, speak it. Never speak what you don't want. We are so used to speaking negatively that it sometimes seems funny to talk like God talks or speak from His perspective. Deuteronomy 30:19 says, "I call heaven and earth to record this day against you, that I have set before you life and death, blessing and cursing: therefore chose life, that both thou and thy seed may live." You choose life or death by the words you speak out of your mouth.

There is a time to talk about what is wrong, like when you go to the doctor and talk about your symptoms, or when you are getting your car repaired. These are current events in your life, and you need to explain what is wrong. What I am talking about is your everyday conversation—what you are saying over and over again to yourself and about your situation.

Introduction

Scriptures on the Power of Words

- **Proverbs 18:21**

  Death and life are in the power of the tongue: and they that love it shall eat the fruit thereof.

- **Matthew 12:36**

  But I say unto you, That every idle word that men shall speak, they shall give account thereof in the day of judgment.

- **Proverbs 21:23**

  Whoso keepeth his mouth and his tongue keepeth his soul from troubles.

- **James 1:26**

  If any man among you seem to be religious, and bridleth not his tongue, but deceiveth his own heart, this man's religion is vain.

- **Proverbs 10:19**

  In the multitude of words there wanteth not sin: but he that refraineth his lips is wise.

- **Matthew 12:37**

  For by thy words thou shall be justified, and by thy words thou shalt be condemned.

- **James 3:5**

  Even so the tongue is a little member, and boasteth great things. Behold, how great a matter a little fire kindleth.

- **Proverbs 11:12**

    He that is void of wisdom despiseth his neighbor: but a man of understanding holdeth his peace.

- **Psalm 141:3**

    Set a watch, O Lord, before my mouth; keep the doors of my lips.

- **Psalm 119:11**

    Thy word have I hid in mine heart, that I might not sin against thee.

*If My people who are called
by My name will humble themselves,
and pray and seek My face, and turn
from their wicked ways, then I will
hear from heaven, and will
forgive their sin
and heal their land.*

—*II Chronicles 7:14 (NKJV)*

Preface

For a long time, my desire to write a prayer book is something I thought about quite often. As I purchased other people's prayer books, it suddenly hit me to write a book of my own.

I love to pray! Even from a little child, I would pray before bed:

Now I lay me down to sleep,
I pray the Lord my soul to keep.
If I should die before I wake,
I pray the Lord my soul to take.

I don't know who told me about praying to God because I didn't grow up in a Christian household. As a child, I would talk to God in a general conversation like talking to a person. Someone instilled in me from my youth the importance of talking to God on a regular basis, and I have been talking/praying to Him ever since.

I am saved now and through the teaching of the Word on prayer, I have learned a lot more about how to pray. The Scriptures in the Bible tell us a lot about praying:

- Philippians 4:6: Be careful for nothing; but in <u>every thing</u> by prayer and supplication with thanksgiving let your requests be known unto God.

- Jeremiah 33:3: Call unto me, and I will answer thee, and shew thee great and mighty things, which thou knowest not.

- Psalm 34:17: The righteous cry, and the Lord heareth, and delivereth them out of all their troubles.

- Matthew 26:41: Watch and pray, that ye enter not into temptation: the spirit indeed is willing, but the flesh is weak.

These are just a few of the many Scriptures on prayer.

I pray this book is a blessing to you and others. Pray these prayers in your daily prayer life and watch how your words begin to frame your world. When you see the change in your life, share this book with others and tell your testimony to encourage them to begin to use God's Word and prayer to change every part of their lives.

In Christ Realities

*The most important belief we possess
is a true knowledge of who God is.*

*The second most important belief is
who we are as children of God, because we cannot
consistently behave in a way that is inconsistent
with how we perceive ourselves.*

—Neil T. Anderson

Who Am I In Christ?

1. World Overcomer—I John 5:4-5
2. More Than a Conqueror—Romans 8:37
3. Heir of God—Romans 8:17
4. God's Workmanship—Ephesians 2:10
5. New Creature—II Corinthians 5:17
6. Righteousness of God—II Corinthians 5:21
7. Ambassador for Christ—II Corinthians 5:20
8. Son—Galatians 4:7
9. Salt of the Earth—Matthew 5:13
10. Victorious through Jesus—I Corinthians 15:57
11. Redeemed—Colossians 1:14
12. Capable—Philippians 4:13
13. Friend of God—John 15:15
14. Child of God—John 1:12
15. Strong—Ephesians 6:10
16. Healed—I Peter 2:24
17. Blessed—Ephesians 1:3
18. Anointed—I John 2:27

19. Of God—I John 4:4

20. Doer of the Word of God—James 1:22

21. Wise—James 1:5

22. Light of the World—Matthew 5:14

23. Loved—I John 4:10

24. Fruit Bearer—John 15:16

25. God's Co-worker—II Corinthians 6:1

PASTOR

And I will give you pastors according to mine heart, which shall feed you with knowledge and understanding.

—Jeremiah 3:15

My Pastor

Father, I thank You that Pastor_____is a gift from You to me and the Body of Christ at _____ (Church), and I recognize, value, honor, and appreciate this gift.

I confess that Pastor_____seeks You daily for wisdom, knowledge, understanding, guidance, and direction. He/she knows Your voice and the voice of satan he/she will not follow. In all his/her ways You are acknowledged, and You are faithful to direct his/her path.

I thank You, Father, that my pastor is a man/woman of prayer and intercedes and covers me and the entire church daily.

You have given me a pastor after Your heart who is faithful to feed the flock with knowledge, understanding, and the full counsel of Your Word. My pastor is a great leader who clearly and accurately casts the vision You have given for our local church. I receive the vision, and run with it. I confess that he/she has every dedicated, willing, and skillful laborer to carry out the vision. Surround my pastor with the right people, and keep my pastor from the wrong people.

Thank You for giving me a caring, sensitive pastor who loves me, the Body of Christ, and all people. My pastor is a godly example to the flock and demonstrates a high degree of excellence, character, integrity, and consistency. No scandal will be a part of my pastor's legacy. Thank You for giving him/

her grace to stand against all temptations, tests, trials, persecution, and false accusations.

Father, I am committed to honor my pastor with my words, finances, submission, and obedience. As a result of my honor to my pastor, I claim Jeremiah 23:4 and confess that I fear no more; I am not dismayed or discouraged; and I do not lack in any need, desire, or good thing, in Jesus' name.

I thank You for my pastor's family. They are a blessing to him/her, to me, and to the Body of Christ. They walk in the fullness of the purpose You have called them to. I honor our first family and esteem and respect them highly. I surround them with prayer, love, protection, and support, and declare no weapon formed against them will prosper, in Jesus' name.

Scripture References

- **II Timothy 4:2**

    Preach the word; be instant in season, out of season; reprove, rebuke, exhort with all longsuffering and doctrine.

- **Acts 20:28**

    Take heed therefore unto yourselves, and to all the flock, over the which the Holy Ghost hath made you overseers, to feed the church of God which he hath purchased with his own blood.

- **Hebrews 13:17**

    Obey them that have the rule over you, and submit yourselves: for they watch for your souls, as that they must give account, that they may do it with joy, and not with grief: for that is profitable for you.

- **James 3:1**

  My brethren, be not many masters, knowing that we shall receive the greater condemnation.

- **Romans 10:14**

  How then shall they call on him in whom they have not believed? and how shall they believe in him of whom they have not heard? and how shall they hear without a preacher?

- **Malachi 2:7**

  For the priest's lips should be knowledge, and they should seek the law at his mouth: for he is the messenger of the Lord of hosts.

- **Acts 6:4**

  But we will give ourselves continually to prayer, and to the ministry of the word.

- **Mark 16:15**

  And he said unto them, Go ye into all the world, and preach the gospel to very creature.

- **Jeremiah 3:15**

  And I will give you pastors according to mine heart, which shall feed you with knowledge and understanding.

LEADERS

A leader is one who knows the way, goes the way, and shows the way.

—John C. Maxwell

Leaders and Volunteers of the Local Church

Father, I thank You that we have every leader and volunteer needed to bring forth Your vision for this ministry. I pray that our leaders are confident, knowledgeable, skillful, passionate, transparent, patient, open-minded, and innovative. They are people of integrity, and they love people.

I pray that You fill our leaders with the knowledge of Your will in all wisdom and spiritual understanding. I pray that those in authority walk worthy of You unto all pleasing, and that they be fruitful in every good work and increasing in the knowledge of You.

Strengthen them with Your will and Your might according to Your glorious power unto all patience and long-suffering with joyfulness. I believe that every leader of _____ walks in "Agape," the unconditional love of God. I thank You that the hearts of those in authority are in Your hands, and their decisions are directed by You.

Father, I lift up every volunteer of _____. I pray they are doing the work of the ministry with joyfulness of heart for You love cheerful givers. I declare that they walk in love, exemplify excellence, and do the ministry by faith, believing You will reward them for their investment into the Kingdom.

I believe that every leader and volunteer has the right attitude, priorities, and motives, and they submit to delegated authority. Our leaders and volunteers demonstrate the fruit of the Spirit—love, joy, peace, longsuffering, gentleness, goodness, meekness, temperance, and faith. We endeavor to keep the unity of the Spirit in the bond of peace, until we all come into the unity of the faith, the knowledge of the Son of God, unto a perfect man.

We are mature in Him, established on the firm foundation of God's Word. We declare and decree that we are a whole body, fitly joined together. Every joint supplies.

Father, You said in Your Word that whatsoever good thing any man does, the same shall he receive of the Lord. So, I ask You to bless all the leaders and volunteers in a personal way. I pray all their needs and desires be granted. I thank You for giving them special favor so that their personal dreams will come to pass.

Thank You, Father, for our leaders and volunteers. Now Holy Spirit, help me to pray God's perfect will, in Jesus' name.

Scripture References

- **Hebrews 6:10 (NASB)**

    For God is not unjust so as to forget your work and the love which you have shown toward His name, by having served and by still serving the saints.

- **Matthew 23:11 (NIV)**

    The greatest among you will be your servant.

- **Mark 10:45**

    For even the Son of man came not to be ministered unto, but to minister, and to give his life a ransom for many.

- **I Peter 4:10**

    As every man hath received the gift, even so minister the same one to another, as good stewards of the manifold grace of God.

- **Matthew 25:40**

    And the King shall answer and say unto them, Verily I say unto you, Inasmuch as ye have done it unto one of the least of these my brethren, ye have done it unto me.

- **I John 3:18**

    My little children, let us not love in word, neither in tongue; but in deed and in truth.

- **Acts 20:35**

    I have shewed you all things, how that so labouring ye ought to support the weak, and to remember the words of the Lord Jesus, how he said, It is more blessed to give than to receive.

- **Ephesians 2:10**

    For we are his workmanship, created in Christ Jesus unto good works, which God hath before ordained that we should walk in them.

- **Galatians 6:10**

    As we have therefore opportunity, let us do good unto all men, especially unto them who are of the household of faith.

LOCAL LEADERSHIP

I alone cannot change the world, but I can cast a stone across the waters to create many ripples.

—*Mother Teresa*

Prayer for the Local Leadership

Father, in Jesus' name, I give thanks for the city of _____ and all the surrounding cities. I hold up in prayer before You those who are seeking positions of authority in our cities. I pray that the Spirit of the Lord rests upon them. I believe that skillful and godly wisdom has entered into the heart of everyone whom You have appointed to lead us. I believe that knowledge is pleasant to them; discretion watches over them; and understanding keeps them and delivers them from the way of evil and from evil men.

Father, I ask that You surround everyone in authority with men and women who are attentive to godly counsel. I believe that they do that which is right in Your sight. I pray that our leaders will be people of integrity who are obedient to Your Word so that we may lead a quiet and peaceable life in all godliness and honesty. I pray that only the upright shall be elected to govern over us and that only people who are blameless and complete in Your sight shall obtain positions of leadership in our city.

Our leaders reject all counsel that violates spiritual principles, trusting God to prove them right. They resist those who would pressure them to violate their conscience.

In the name of Jesus, I take authority over every evil attempt to corrupt or create unfairness in every election. I take authority over the spirit of division, racial prejudice, slander, and every evil spirit that tries to come against Your chosen candidate in this election. I confess that every voter will come out to vote and seek Your face concerning the candidate that You have chosen to lead our city.

It is written in Your Word that the heart of the king is in the hand of the Lord, and You turn it whichever way You desire. I believe that the hearts of leaders are in Your hands, and that their decisions are divinely directed by You, Lord.

Lord, keep this city under Your care. I declare that Jesus is Lord over the city of_____, in Jesus' name.

Scripture References

- **Psalm 78:72**

    So he fed them according to the integrity of his heart; and guided them by the skilfulness of his hands.

- **Philippians 2:4**

    Look not every man on his own things, but every man also on the things of others.

- **Galatians 6:9**

    And let us not be weary in well doing: for in due season we shall reap, if we faint not.

- **Isaiah 41:10**

    Fear thou not; for I am with thee: be not dismayed; for I am thy God: I will strengthen thee; yea, I will help thee; yea, I will uphold thee with the right hand of my righteousness.

- **I Peter 2:17**

  Honour all men. Love the brotherhood. Fear God. Honour the king.

- **Romans 13:1**

  Let every soul be subject unto the higher powers. For there is no power but of God: the powers that be are ordained of God.

- **Proverbs 21:1**

  The king's heart is in the hand of the Lord, as the rivers of water: he turneth it whithersoever he will.

BODY OF CHRIST

The kingdom of God is not going to be advanced by our churches being filled with men, but by men in our churches being filled with God.

—Duncan Campbell

Prayer for the Body of Christ (Universal and Local)

Dear Father, I pray and confess Your Word over the Body of Christ. Give to us the spirit of wisdom and revelation in the knowledge of You. Enlightened the eyes of our understanding so that we may know what the hope of Your calling is and the riches of Your glorious inheritance in us, the saints. Help us to know and walk in the resurrected power of our Lord Jesus, the power You demonstrated when You raised Him from the dead.

Strengthen us with all might by Your Spirit in our inner man so that we will be rooted and grounded in Your love.

I lift up in prayer Your ordained and called leadership of_____, the apostle, prophet, evangelist, pastor, and teacher. Help them to be examples of the believers in word, conversation, love, spirit, faith, faithfulness, and purity.

Through their leadership, I pray that the saints be perfected and equipped to do the work of the ministry, and the Body of Christ be edified.

Father, help us believers worldwide to come into the unity of the faith, the full knowledge of Christ and who we are in Christ, and spiritual maturity both in character and power. As Your ambassadors in the earth, give us boldness to preach and teach Your Word, not with enticing words of man's wisdom, but in demonstration of the Holy Spirit and of power.

We desire to grow and develop in the fruit of the Spirit and operate proficiently and effectually in the gifts of the Spirit.

Thank You for giving us the grace to be salt and light in the earth and to glorify You in all that we do, in Jesus' name.

Scripture References

- **Romans 12:4-5**

  [4] For as we have many members in one body, and all members have not the same office: [5] So we, being many, are one body in Christ, and every one members one of another.

- **I Corinthians 12:27**

  Now ye are the body of Christ, and members in particular.

- **Ephesians 4:4**

  There is one body, and one Spirit, even as ye are called in one hope of your calling.

- **Ephesians 1:22**

  And hath put all things under his feet, and gave him to be the head over all things to the church.

- **I Corinthians 12:12**

  For as the body is one, and hath many members, and all the members of that one body, being many, are one body: so also is Christ.

- **I Corinthians 12:14**

  For the body is not one member, but many.

- **Galatians 3:27**

  For as many of you have been baptized into Christ have put on Christ.

- **Ephesians 4:25**

  Wherefore putting away lying, speak every man truth with his neighbour: for we are members one of another.

- **Colossians 1:24**

  Who now rejoice in my sufferings for you, and fill up that which is behind of the afflictions of Christ in my flesh for his body's sake, which is the church.

- **Ephesians 5:23**

  For the husband is the head of the wife, even as Christ is the head of the church: and he is the saviour of the body.

The Lost

*For the Son of man is come to seek
and to save that which was lost.*

—Jesus

Prayer for the Lost

Father, I pray for the lost in Jesus' name. Your Word says that You are not willing that any should perish, but that all should come to repentance. I know that the harvest is plenteous, but the laborers are few. I pray that You, Lord of the harvest, send forth laborers that are full of Your Word and full of compassion. Send us Lord! Send me! I pray that Your Word have free course and not be hindered by any satanic force or power. Open a door of utterance for me. I pray that the lost give attention to Your Word and that their eyes be opened to the truth about their lost condition. I pray that they receive Jesus Christ as their Lord and Savior, and come into the full knowledge of the truth.

Now, satan, I bind you, every ruling spirit of darkness, and every strategy designed to keep the lost from the truth in Jesus' name. Go ministering spirits (angels of the living God) and bring in the harvest. I call the harvest in from the north, south, west, and east in Jesus' name.

Father, I thank You for answering my prayers, and I rejoice with all of heaven as multitudes all over the earth are being saved, in Jesus' name.

Scripture References

- **Romans 10:1**

    Brethren, my heart's desire and prayer to God for Israel is, that they might be saved.

- **I Timothy 2:4**

  Who will have all men to be saved, and to come unto the knowledge of the truth.

- **II Timothy 2:26**

  And that they may recover themselves out of the snare of the devil, who was taken captive by him at his will.

- **I John 5:14**

  And this is the confidence that we have in him, that, if we ask anything according to his will, he heareth us.

- **John 3:16**

  For God so loved the world, that he gave his only begotten Son, that whosoever believeth in him should not perish, but have everlasting life.

- **Ezekiel 36:26**

  A new heart also will I give you, and a new spirit will I put within you: and I will take away the stony heart out of your flesh, and I will give you a heart of flesh.

- **John 6:44**

  No man can come to me, except the Father which hath sent me draw him: and I will raise him up at the last day.

- **Colossians 1:13**

  Who hath delivered us from the power of darkness, and hath translated us into the kingdom of his dear Son.

- **I Corinthians 2:14**

    But the natural man receiveth not the things of the Spirit of God: for they are foolishness unto him: neither can he know them, because they are spiritually discerned.

- **John 14:6**

    Jesus saith unto him, I am the way, the truth, and the life; no man cometh unto the Father, but by me.

Armed Forces and Military Personnel

He loves his country best who strives to make it best.

—Robert Ingersoll

Armed Forces and Military Personnel

Father, I pray for our Armed Forces—those in the Navy, Marines, Air Force, Coast Guard, Reserves, and all other military personnel. I pray for the safety of all our military personnel, and I plead the Blood of Jesus over them. I declare that the men and women who serve in the Armed Forces dwell in the secret place of the Most High and abide under the shadow of the Almighty. Thousands may fall around them, but destruction does not come near them. I thank You that You make our enemies to be at peace with us at all times.

The Lord has given His angels charge over them, their spouses, and children. I declare that no evil comes near them, and no plague comes near their dwelling.

I take authority over terrorism and every threat against democracy in our country and abroad. No weapon formed shall prosper. I resist fear, frustration, and anxiety, and surround our Armed Forces with faith, peace, and love.

Father, provide for and protect the families of those who are serving in the Armed Forces. I pray that their families are undergirded, uplifted, and edified. They lack no good thing because God supplies all their needs. They are whole (nothing missing, nothing broken, and nothing lacking in their lives).

Father, for those that do not know you, I pray for laborers in the Armed Forces to share the Good News of the Gospel to our troops so that they can make You Savior and Lord over their lives.

I thank You for these men and women putting their lives in danger for us. I thank You for watching over Your Word to perform it. Now, Holy Spirit, help me to pray for our military and their families, in Jesus' name.

Scripture References

- **Psalm 29:11**

    The Lord will give strength unto his people; the Lord will bless his people with peace.

- **Joshua 1:9**

    Have not I commanded the? Be strong and of good courage; be not afraid, neither be thou dismayed: for the Lord thy God is with thee withersoever thou goest.

- **Psalm 46:1**

    God is our refuge and strength, a very present help in trouble.

- **Psalm 91:14**

    Because he hath set his love upon me, therefore will I deliver him: I will set him on high, because he hath known my name.

- **Psalm 91:1**

    He that dwelleth in the secret place of the Most High shall abide under the shadow of the Almighty.

- **Deuteronomy 31:6**

    Be strong and of good courage, fear not, nor be afraid of them: for the Lord thy God, he it is that doth go with thee; he will not fail thee, nor forsake thee.

- **Psalm 27:1**

    The Lord is my light and my salvation; whom shall I fear? The Lord is the strength of my life; of whom shall I be afraid?

- **II Timothy 1:7**

    For God has not given us the spirit of fear, but of power, and of love, and of a sound mind.

- **Psalm 56:3**

    What time I am afraid, I will trust in thee.

- **II Samuel 22:4**

    I will call on the Lord, who is worthy to be praised: so shall I be saved from mine enemies.

INDIVIDUAL MEMBERS OF YOUR CHURCH

God wants every member of the Body of Christ to be a blessing one to another; that's why, everyone has to be involved in the Ministry.

—Sunday Adelaja

Individual Members of Your Church

Father, in the name of Jesus, I pray for every member of_____, every baby, child, teen, and adult.

I pray that the Word of God grows daily in each life. We are doers of the Word and not just hearers only. I believe that the fruit of the Spirit is developed in each life; that the gifts of the Spirit are in manifestation in each life; and that Christ be formed in each life.

Father, I believe that each member is faithfully fulfilling his/her role in the local church and in the world. We are examples of Christ, ministering the Good News of the Gospel everywhere we go. Every member is redeemed from sickness and disease. We live long upon the earth; every member lives a minimum of 70 years, and if not satisfied, 120 years. We take care of our bodies through rest, exercise, proper diet, and drinking water. Our bodies are the temple of the Holy Spirit.

I believe that Jesus took the punishment in His mind so that we may have peace. I declare that we have the mind of Christ and the peace of God guards our hearts and minds. We refuse to worry because we cast all our cares on the Lord. We are healed of all emotional and mental deficiencies. There is nothing missing, and nothing broken in our bodies or in our minds.

I believe all our members have healthy, loving, and respectful relationships. Husbands and wives have mutually fulfilling marriages. Parents are raising their children up in the nurture and admonition of the Lord. Our children are the seed of the righteous. They are delivered from negative peer pressure. They are fulfilling their purposes in the Lord. All of our members—married, single, young, and old—are walking in the blessings of the Lord, fulfilling their purposes, and impacting their world for Christ.

I believe every member of_____is a tither and a giver. We are enjoying the windows of Heaven's blessings, and we have provision from expected and unexpected resources. Every need is met, and we have abundance and no lack. God is our source, and He gives us seed to sow. We have more than enough to give. Because we are tithers, the devourer is rebuked for our sake.

Father, I believe no weapon formed against_____ or its members shall prosper. I plead the Blood of Jesus over_____and its members. A thousand shall fall at our side and ten thousand at our right hand, but no evil shall come near our dwelling. I believe our members are redeemed from identify theft, accidents, car jackings, murder, crime, rape, and all forms of evil. I pray that You don't take us out of the world, but that You keep us from the evil in the world. I loose the angels of God over our church and its members.

Father, I thank You for blessing each member to labor with supernatural ability and at a high level of excellence and integrity. I thank You for causing promotion and favor on our jobs. We have doors of opportunity open to us that no man can shut. Others are using their resources, abilities, and influence on our behalf.

I believe that every member of_____is enjoying good Christian fellowship with other believers, in Jesus' name.

Scripture References

- **I Corinthians 12:27**

  Now ye are the body of Christ, and members in particular.

- **Ephesians 1:22**

  And hath put all things under his feet, and gave him to be the head over all things to the church.

- **John 17:15**

  I pray not that thou shouldest take them out of the world, but thou shouldest keep them from the evil.

- **Psalm 91:15**

  He shall call upon me, and I will answer him: I will be with him in trouble; I will deliver him, and honour him.

- **Psalm 91:16**

  With long life will I satisfy him, and shew him my salvation.

- **Psalm 103:3**

  Who forgiveth all thine iniquities; who healeth all thy diseases.

Individual Members of Your Church

- **Psalm 91:10**

  There shall no evil befall thee, neither shall any plague come nigh thy dwelling.

- **Isaiah 54:17**

  No weapon that is formed against thee shall prosper; and every tongue that shall rise against thee in judgment thou shalt condemn.

- **I Corinthians 12:18**

  But now hath God set the members every one of them in the body, as it hath pleased him.

- **Philippians 4:19**

  But my God shall supply all your need according to his riches in glory by Christ Jesus.

NATION

*If we forget that we are One Nation Under God,
then we will be a nation gone under.*

—*Ronald Reagan*

NATION

"Let everyone be subject to the governing authorities, for there is no authority except that God has established. The authorities that exist have been established by God." (Romans 13:1 NIV)

You said to pray for all those in authority so that we could live a quiet and peaceful life. Father, I pray that You fill our President, Vice President, his cabinet, and all government officials with the knowledge of Your will in all wisdom and spiritual understanding. I pray that those in authority walk worthy of You unto all pleasing, that they be fruitful in every good work, and increasing in the knowledge of You. Strengthen them with Your will and Your might according to Your glorious power unto all patience and long suffering with joyfulness. Father, I believe that the hearts of those in authority are in Your hands, and their decisions are directed by You.

Our leaders walk in godly wisdom, and they surround themselves with godly advisors who will advise them in the way of righteousness. I pray that You will turn the hearts of our leaders to Your purposes.

I pray that God will reveal the deep things of darkness in this nation and bring utter darkness into the light.

We are victorious in our fight against terrorism and no weapon formed against this nation shall prosper. I pray that You expose anyone or anything that is not right. I plead the Blood of Jesus over this nation, and I declare that Jesus is Lord over the United States of America.

I undergird our leaders in prayer, and I will not allow any corrupt communication to proceed out of my mouth concerning those whom God has placed in positions of authority.

Now, Holy Spirit, help me to pray God's perfect will for our President, his cabinet, and government officials, in Jesus' name, amen.

Scripture References

- **II Chronicles 7:14**

    If my people, which are called by my name, shall humble themselves, and pray, and seek my face, and turn from their wicked ways; then will I hear from heaven, and will forgive their sin, and will heal their land.

- **Proverbs 21:1**

    The king's heart is in the hand of the Lord, as the rivers of water: he turneth it withersoever he will.

- **Psalm 2:10-11**

    [10] Be wise now therefore, O ye kings: be instructed, ye judges of the earth. [11] Serve the LORD with fear, and rejoice with trembling.

- **Proverbs 11:14**

    Where no counsel is, the people fall: but in the multitude of counsellors there is safety.

- **Numbers 23:24a**

    Behold, the people shall rise up as a great lion.

- **Isaiah 49:6**

    And he said, It is a light thing that thou shouldest be my servant to raise up the tribes of Jacob, and to restore the preserved of Israel: I will also give thee for a light to the Gentiles, that thou mayest be my salvation unto the end of the earth.

- **Proverbs 3:3-5**

    [4] Let not mercy and truth forsake thee: bind them about thy neck; write them upon the table of thine heart: [4] So shalt thou find favour and good understanding in the sight of God and man. [5] Trust in the LORD with all thine heart; and lean not unto thine own understanding.

- **Jeremiah 29:7**

    And seek the peace of the city whither I have caused you to be carried away captives, and pray unto the Lord for it: for in peace thereof shall ye have peace.

- **Romans 13:1**

    Let every soul be subject unto the higher powers. For there is no power but of God: the powers that be are ordained of God.

SALVATION

*The worst mistake a man can make
is to miss heaven and go to hell.*

*—Phineas Coleman
(Kennetha Moore's Grandfather)*

Salvation

Father, I recognize that I have not been living my life for You. I need You in my life. I believe that Jesus died for my sins on the cross, and He was raised from the dead so that I might be right with You. I ask Your forgiveness for my sins, and I receive Your forgiveness for them. I ask You to come into my life now and become Lord over my life. From this day forward, I promise to allow Your Word to govern my life. Help me to follow Your leading the rest of my life. Thank You for coming into my heart, in Jesus' name, amen.

Next Steps for New Believers

Don't expect a change in your actions and thoughts overnight. You have to grow up in Christ just like a newborn baby has to grow into an adult. Your spirit man was born again, not your flesh. Growth takes time through reading, prayer, church attendance, and listening to God's Word. Here is a list of next steps that will be helpful to you as a new believer.

1. Ask God to guide you to a church where the pastor loves his flock, teaches the Word of God, and shows you how to apply it to your everyday life.

Why do I need to attend church?

   a. To fellowship with other Christians (Acts 2:42)

   b. To be a supplying part of the Body of Christ (Ephesians 4:16)

   c. To grow in the Word of God (I Peter 2:2)

d. God instructed us to not forsake the assembly of ourselves together (Hebrews 10:23-25)

   e. Isolation is not God's order (Hebrews 10:23-25)

   f. To worship God corporately (John 4:23-24)

   g. Pastors are a gift to believers (Ephesians 4:11-12)
   You can't enjoy the gift if you are not connected.

2. Get water-baptized (Mark 16:16)

   Baptism is an outward expression of your commitment to God.

3. Get filled with the Spirit with the Bible evidence of speaking in tongues (Acts 1:4-8)

   Note: The baptism with the Holy Spirit is an experience after salvation that equips the believer with power to serve.

4. Get in discipleship classes

5. Serve in the local church (Ephesians 4:16)

6. Share your faith (Acts 1:8)

Scripture References

- **Acts 4:12**

    Neither is there salvation in any other: for there is none other name under heaven given among men, whereby we must be saved.

- **Act 16:31**

    And they said, Believe on the Lord Jesus Christ, and thou shalt be saved, and thy house.

- **Psalm 62:1**

    Truly my soul waiteth upon God; from him cometh my salvation.

- **Acts 2:21**

    And it shall come to pass, that whosoever shall call on the name of the Lord shall be saved.

- **Romans 10:10**

    For with the heart man believeth unto righteousness; and with the mouth confession is made unto salvation.

- **Luke 19:10**

    For the Son of Man is come to seek and to save that which was lost.

- **Romans 1:16**

For I am not ashamed of the gospel of Christ: for it is the power of God unto salvation to every one that believeth; to the Jew first, and also to the Greek.

- **I Corinthians 15:22**

For as in Adam all die, even so in Christ shall all be made alive.

- **John 3:16**

For God so loved the world, that he gave his only begotten Son, that whosoever believeth in him should not perish, but have everlasting life.

- **II Timothy 1:9**

Who hath saved us, and called us with an holy calling, not according to our works, but according to his own purpose and grace, which was given us in Christ Jesus before the world began.

Spiritual Growth

Becoming like Christ is a long, slow process of growth.

—Rick Warren

*When I was a child, I spake as a child,
I understood as a child, I thought as a child,
but when I became a man,
I put away childish things.*

—I Corinthians 13:11

SPIRITUAL GROWTH

Thank You, Father, for saving me, for allowing me to be Your child, and for making me a member of Your family. I am a new creature in Christ, and the old things of my life before accepting You are passed away. Now as Your child, I desire to grow up into spiritual maturity. You said that I am to desire Your Word so that I may grow. Work within me both the desire and ability to set and keep godly priorities. Help me to be a diligent student of the Word of God and allow its instructions, principles, and wisdom to govern my life. I desire to be a doer of the Word and not just a hearer.

Father, I know that You desire intimacy with me, and I rejoice in Your love for me. Give me the grace to commit to a daily time of prayer and fellowship with You. I declare that I will not be negligent to offer You the worship You rightly deserve. Help me to worship You in spirit and in truth.

I receive Your daily guidance and leadership. The Holy Spirit lives in me, and I am His temple—His dwelling place. You sent Him to teach me and guide me in all truth. I receive You Holy Spirit, and I declare You are more than capable of assisting me and helping me to be successful in life. I am an overcomer because of Your presence in my life. I can do all things because You strengthen me. I know Your voice and the voice of a stranger I will not follow.

Father, give me the compassion and boldness to declare and share with others the things You teach me. I believe I am growing up in Christ and pleasing my Father, in Jesus' name.

SPIRITUAL GROWTH

Scripture References

- **I Peter 2:2**

    As newborn babes, desire the sincere milk of the word, that you may grow thereby.

- **I Thessalonians 3:12**

    And the Lord make you to increase and abound in love one toward another, and toward all men, even as we do toward you.

- **Ephesians 4:15**

    But speaking the truth in love, may grow up into him in all things, which is the head, even Christ.

- **I Samuel 2:26**

    And the child Samuel grew on, and was in favour both with the Lord, and also with men.

- **Colossians 1:10**

    That ye might walk worthy of the Lord unto all pleasing, being fruitful in every good work, and increasing in the knowledge of God.

- **II Peter 1:5-7**

    [5] And beside this, giving all diligence, add to your faith virtue; and to virtue knowledge; [6] And to knowledge temperance; and to temperance patience; and to patience godliness; [7] And to godliness brotherly kindness; and to brotherly kindness charity.

- **II Thessalonians 1:3**

    We are bound to thank God always for you, brethren, as it is meet, because that your faith groweth exceedingly, and the charity of every one of you all toward each other aboundeth.

- **II Peter 3:18**

    But grow in grace, and in the knowledge of our Lord and Saviour Jesus Christ. To him be glory both now and for ever. Amen.

- **Luke 2:52**

    And Jesus increased in wisdom and stature, and in favour with God and man.

- **Matthew 5:6**

    Blessed are they which do hunger and thirst after righteousness: for they shall be filled.

Believing for a Mate

Choose your life's mate carefully.

From this one decision will come 90% of all your happiness or misery.

—H. Jackson Brown, Jr.

Believing for a Mate

Father, I thank You for raising up a generation of single men and women who love You and are committed to Your Word. I believe that there are godly single men and women whose minds are being transformed by Your Word. They are capable of committing to marriage as You designed and ordained marriage in Your Word.

Father, You said in Your Word that in order to avoid fornication, every man should have his own wife and every woman should have her own husband. You also said to drink waters out of our own cisterns and running water out of our own wells and not out of the cisterns and wells of strangers.

Based on Your Word, Father, I desire to be married and have a spiritually compatible companion. I know that "oneness" is Your plan for marriage. I desire a godly, loving, and emotionally healthy person so that we together will walk in a shared vision and fulfill Your purpose for our lives. I desire someone that desires me and is willing to work for spiritual, emotional, and physical intimacy. I pray that we be physically attracted to each other, and we have and enjoy a mutually fulfilling sexual relationship. I desire to be governed by Your Word, and I want someone who will allow the Word of God to govern us even during conflict and difficult situations.

I am redeemed from evil and will not enter into or experience an abusive, controlling, or selfish relationship.

Father, order my steps in selecting both who to date and marry. Help me to be led by Your Spirit and not lean to my own understanding or fleshly emotions.

Help me to grow up daily in the things of God. Reveal any weaknesses or deficiencies in my life that I need to work on now. Help me to be a great marriage partner. I believe I receive, in Jesus' name.

Scripture References

- **Mark 11:24**

  Therefore I say unto you, What things soever ye desire, when ye pray, believe that ye receive them, and ye shall have them.

- **Philippians 4:6**

  Be careful for nothing; but in every thing by prayer and supplication with thanksgiving let your requests be made known unto God.

- **Matthew 7:7**

  Ask, and it shall be given you; seek, and ye shall find; knock, and it shall be opened unto you.

- **Genesis 2:18**

  And the Lord God said, It is not good that the man should be alone; I will make him an help meet for him.

- **Jeremiah 29:11**

  For I know the thoughts that I think toward you, saith the Lord, thoughts of peace, and not of evil, to give you an expected end.

- **Romans 15:13**

  Now the God of hope fill you with all joy and peace in believing, that ye may abound in hope, through the power of the Holy Ghost.

- **Matthew 6:33**

  But seek ye first the kingdom of God, and his righteousness; and all these things shall be added unto you.

- **Psalm 37:4-5**

  ⁴ Delight thyself also in the Lord: and he shall give thee the desires of thine heart. ⁵ Commit thy way unto the Lord; trust also in him; and he shall bring it to pass.

- **Proverbs 18:22**

  Whoso findeth a wife findeth a good thing, and obtaineth favour of the Lord.

- **Genesis 2:24**

  Therefore shall a man leave his father and his mother, and shall cleave unto his wife: and they shall be one flesh.

MARRIAGE

A successful marriage requires falling in love many times, always with the same person.

—Mignon McLaughlin

Marriage

Father, in the name of Jesus, I pray for my marriage today. I pray that You would protect my marriage from anything that would try to harm or destroy it.

Shield my marriage from selfishness and neglect, from the evil plans of the enemy, and from unhealthy, addictive, and dangerous situations. I resist any thoughts of infidelity in our marriage. My spouse and I are attracted to each other physically and emotionally, and we keep our bodies in good physical shape. We have affection for each other, and we are sexually fulfilled. We are affectionate in our gestures and our words. I confess my marriage is free from past hurts, negative emotions, and unrealistic expectations of each other. We have open and honest communication, and we both listen to what each other has to say. I don't assume that my spouse knows how I feel or what I want. We are ready and willing to consider things from each other's point of view. We don't go to bed mad at each other, and we resolve conflict quickly even if we agree to disagree. When we disagree, we invite God to become involved in our decision-making, and He guides us in the direction we should go.

We walk in the fruit of the Spirit in our marriage. We walk in love, joy, peace, kindness, goodness, faithfulness, gentleness, and self-control.

We have a social life together, and we enjoy spending time with each other on a regular basis. My spouse is my best friend. We enjoy shared activities and companionship. We set aside time to talk to each other, vacation, and do fun activities together. Our marriage is united in the bond of friendship, commitment, generosity, and mutual understanding. Love is displayed in full expression, and we are knit together in truth. We support each other and have each other's back. We believe that God is working in our marriage what is pleasing in His sight.

No weapon formed against my marriage shall prosper. I declare that my marriage is fulfilling, and it grows stronger day-by-day because it is founded on the Word of God and rooted and grounded in love.

Now Holy Spirit, I thank You for helping me to pray for my marriage, in Jesus' name.

Scripture References

- **Ephesians 5:22-33**

    [22] Wives, submit yourselves unto your own husbands, as unto the Lord. [23] For the husband is the head of the wife, even as Christ is the head of the church: and he is the saviour of the body. [24] Therefore as the church is subject unto Christ, so let the wives be to their own husbands in every thing. [25] Husbands, love your wives, even as Christ also loved the church, and gave himself for it; [26] That he might sanctify and cleanse it with the washing of water by the word, [27] That he might present it to himself a glorious church, not having spot, or wrinkle, or any such thing; but that it should be holy and without blemish. [28] So ought men to love their wives as their own bodies. He that loveth his wife

loveth himself. ²⁹ For no man ever yet hated his own flesh; but nourisheth and cherisheth it, even as the Lord the church: ³⁰ For we are members of his body, of his flesh, and of his bones. ³¹ For this cause shall a man leave his father and mother, and shall be joined unto his wife, and they two shall be one flesh. ³² This is a great mystery: but I speak concerning Christ and the church. ³³ Nevertheless let every one of you in particular so love his wife even as himself; and the wife see that she reverence her husband.

- **Genesis 2:24**

Therefore shall a man leave his father and his mother, and shall cleave unto his wife: and they shall be one flesh.

- **Proverbs 18:22**

Whoso findeth a wife findeth a good thing, and obtaineth favour of the LORD.

- **Hebrews 13:4**

Marriage is honourable in all, and the bed undefiled; but whoremongers and adulterers God will judge.

- **Proverbs 21:9**

It is better to dwell in a corner of the housetop, than with a brawling woman in a wide house.

- **Proverbs 19:14**

House and riches are the inheritance of fathers: and a prudent wife is from the Lord.

- **I Corinthians 13:4-10**

    ⁴ Charity suffereth long, and is kind; charity envieth not; charity vaunteth not itself, is not puffed up, ⁵ Doth not behave itself unseemly, seeketh not her own, is not easily provoked, thinketh no evil; ⁶ Rejoiceth not in iniquity, but rejoiceth in the truth; ⁷ Beareth all things, believeth all things, hopeth all things, endureth all things. ⁸ Charity never faileth: but whether there be prophecies, they shall fail; whether there be tongues, they shall cease; whether there be knowledge, it shall vanish away. ⁹ For we know in part, and we prophesy in part. ¹⁰ But when that which is perfect is come, then that which is in part shall be done away.

- **II Corinthians 6:14**

    Be ye not unequally yoked together with unbelievers: for what fellowship hath righteousness with unrighteousness? And what communion hath light with darkness?

- **Ephesians 5:31**

    For this cause shall a man leave his father and mother, and shall be joined unto his wife, and they two shall be one flesh.

- **Ephesians 5:25**

    Husbands, love your wives, even as Christ also loved the church, and gave himself for it.

- **Ephesians 5:33**

  Nevertheless let every one of you in particular so love his wife even as himself; and the wife see that she reverence her husband.

- **Proverbs 18:22 (NIV)**

  He who finds a wife finds what is good and receives favor from the Lord.

7 Tips for Improving Communication in Your Relationship[1]

1. Be intentional about spending time together.
2. Use more "I" statements and less "you" statements.
3. Be specific.
4. Avoid mind reading.
5. Express negative feelings constructively.
6. Listen without being defensive.
7. Freely express positive feelings.

---

[1] FirstThings.org – August 16, 2017

FAMILY

A happy family is but an earlier heaven.

—*George Bernard Shaw*

Family

Father, in the name of Jesus, I lift up in prayer my immediate and extended family. I claim the salvation of my whole household, and I pray that You, the Lord of the harvest, send forth laborers to share the gospel with each member of my family. I believe that they are all open to the truth and give attention to Your Word. Thank You for opening their eyes and helping them to see clearly. Satan, your power and influence over my family are broken in the name of Jesus. Take your hands off of them now! Angels, you are released to position my family members to hear the Gospel. I believe my family members are receiving Jesus as Lord, and I declare Jesus is Lord over my household.

My household is built upon godly wisdom. We have the mind of Christ and acknowledge God daily to direct our lives. My family is strong in the Lord and the power of His might, and we are of good courage. We put the Word of God first place in our home, and we hold fast to our confession of faith. We are doers of the Word of God and not hearers only. We are examples of the Believers in our word, conversation, charity, faith, manner of life, and purity. The fruit of the Spirit—love, joy, peace, forbearance, kindness, goodness, faithfulness, gentleness, and self-control—is developing in our lives. Our minds are renewed with God's Word, and we no longer live the way we did when we were unsaved. We walk in integrity, and our children are blessed after us. We demonstrate in our lives the good, acceptable, and perfect will of God.

My family walks in divine health. Jesus took our infirmities and bore our sicknesses, and with His stripes, we are healed. Sickness and disease shall not come near our dwelling. Each member of my family lives a long, strong, and healthy life. We all live out our full days, and no one will die prematurely.

Jesus Christ is our source. The blessing of the Lord is on my family, and we walk in His riches and wealth. We are tithers and givers, and we experience the windows of Heaven's blessing. All our bills are paid on time; we ride prosperously; we dress sharper than the lilies; and we are blessed to be a blessing. God is our Source, and we live an abundant, debt-free life. We are blessed of God, and we are a blessing to others.

My family is rooted and grounded in the love of God. We walk in unity and work diligently to keep peace. We choose lowliness, meekness, longsuffering, and forbearance. We let no corrupt communication proceed out of our mouths, but only good communication that ministers grace. We don't accept bitterness, wrath, clamor, and evil speaking to govern our lives. We esteem each other and care about the welfare of each family member. We are kind, tenderhearted, and forgiving even as Christ forgave us.

We claim Psalm 91 and Psalm 34:7 over our household. We declare the angels of God encamp around us to protect us from all hurt, harm, or danger. God has not given us the spirit of fear, but of power, love, and a sound mind. We will not be afraid of the destruction all around us. It shall not come near us. We are in the world, but we are kept from the evil in the world.

Thank you, Father, for watching over Your Word to perform it. Now, Holy Spirit, I trust You to help me to pray for my family, in Jesus' name.

Scripture References

- **I Timothy 3:5**

  For if a man know not how to rule his own house, how shall he take care of the church of God?

- **Proverbs 22:6**

  Train up a child in the way he should go: and when he is old, he will not depart from it.

- **Exodus 20:12**

  Honour thy father and thy mother: that thy days may be long upon the land which the Lord thy God giveth thee.

- **Genesis 2:24**

  Therefore shall a man leave his father and his mother, and shall cleave unto his wife: and they shall be one flesh.

- **Colossians 3:19**

  Husbands, love your wives, and be not bitter against them.

- **Genesis 18:19**

  For I know him, that he will command his children and his household after him, and they shall keep the way of the LORD, to do justice and judgment; that the Lord may bring upon Abraham that which he hath spoken of him.

- **Acts 16:31**

  And they said, Believe on the Lord Jesus Christ, and thou shalt be saved, and thy house.

- **Ephesians 5:21**

  Submit yourselves one to another in the fear of God.

- **Acts 10:2**

  A devout man, and one that feared God with all his house, which gave much alms to the people, and prayed to God alway.

- **I Timothy 5:8**

  But if any provide not for his own, and specially for those of his own house, he hath denied the faith, and is worse than an infidel.

PREGNANCY

*A baby fills a place in your heart
that you never knew was empty.*

—*Author Unknown*

Pregnancy

Children are a gift and a reward from the Lord. Therefore, in the name of Jesus, I desire a healthy pregnancy of nine months with no complications for me and my unborn child. I resist fatigue, spotting, morning sickness, moodiness, and problems with sleeping. My family and I will have an enjoyable experience with this pregnancy. I call the fruit of my womb blessed, and nothing shall cause me to miscarry or cast my baby prematurely.

I will get plenty of rest, drink water to hydrate my body, and watch my diet in order to not gain an excessive amount of weight. Every organ, gland, cell, and tissue of my body functions throughout this pregnancy in perfection the way God created it to function. At each week of pregnancy, my child is developing the way he/she should. My baby's eyes, ears, nose, mouth, skin, organs, feet, arms, and bones are all in perfect condition. I plead the Blood of Jesus over me and my child. I say no weapon formed against us shall prosper. A thousand shall fall at our side, ten thousand at our right hands, but it shall not come near us. We are redeemed from all forms of destruction, accidents, trauma, and disease. I loose the angels of God over me and my baby to protect us and keep us.

I will have a quick, painless, easy vaginal birth with no complications. My baby will be born headfirst, not breech or face down.

In Jesus' name, I declare I won't tear during delivery. I will remain relaxed, stress free, and worry-free because I know the Lord is with me. He will never leave me or forsake me.

This is the Lord's doing, and it is a blessing to see, in Jesus' name, amen.

Scripture References

- **I Peter 5:7**

    Casting all your care upon him; for he careth for you.

- **Philippians 4:13**

    I can do all things through Christ which strengtheneth me.

- **Psalm 139:13-14**

    [13] For thou hast possessed my reins: thou hast covered me in my mother's womb. [14] I will praise thee; for I am fearfully and wonderfully made: marvellous are thy works; and that my soul knoweth right well.

- **Psalm 22:9-10**

    [9] But thou art he that took me out of the womb: thou didst make me hope when I was upon my mother's breasts. [10] I was cast upon thee from the womb: thou art my God from my mother's belly.

- **Psalm 112:7**

    He shall not be afraid of evil tidings: his heart is fixed, trusting in the Lord.

- **Jeremiah 1:5**

    Before I formed thee in the belly I knew thee; and before thou camest forth out of the womb I sanctified thee, and I ordained thee a prophet unto the nations.

- **Psalm 127:3-4**

    ³ Lo, children are an heritage of the LORD: and the fruit of the womb is his reward. ⁴ As arrows are in the hand of a mighty man; so are children of the youth.

- **Psalm 71:6**

    By thee have I been holden up from the womb: thou art he that took me out of my mother's bowels: my praise shall be continually of thee.

- **Isaiah 41:10**

    Fear thou not; for I am with thee: be not dismayed; for I am thy God: I will strengthen thee; yea, I will help thee; yea, I will uphold thee with the right hand of my righteousness.

CHILDREN

*It is easier to build strong children
than to repair broken men.*

—Frederick Douglass

*A man must talk to God about his children
before he talks to his children about God.*

—Ed Cole

Confession About Your Children

Father, in Jesus' name, I speak Your Word over my children today.

I declare that my children are mighty in the earth. They are trained up in the ways of the Lord, and when they are old, they will not depart. They have knowledge and skill in all learning and wisdom. In all matters of wisdom and understanding, they are ten times smarter than all others. They are the head in their classes and not the tail, above only and not beneath. They have favor with the principal, the teachers, and the other students. They are calm, cool, collected, and knowledgeable in test environments. They always score high on tests and entrance exams.

They do not succumb to the ungodly pressure of their peers. They are not ashamed of God, His Word, and serving Him. They are growing and becoming strong in spirit, filled with wisdom, and the grace of God is upon them. They are increasing in wisdom, stature, and favor with God and man.

They have good, healthy, Christ-centered self-esteem. They know who they are in Christ, and they don't feel the need to conform or be like others. They feel good in their own skin and in who Christ created them to be. They are leaders and not just followers. They set their own trends and styles.

They respect their parents and others in authority so that they can live a long life.

Children

They hear God's voice, listen to godly wisdom, and make good decisions. They learn from others' mistakes and avoid making the same mistakes for themselves.

They are redeemed from drugs, alcohol, bullying, illicit sex, gangs, perversion, pornography, bad company, witchcraft, and cigarettes. They use social media in a wise way, and they don't compromise their future.

They will not experience sexual molestation, pedophilia, incest, or gang or date rape. No evil comes near their dwelling.

I (parent) am a good example to my children. I love them dearly, and they have no need to feel unwanted, unloved, or rejected. The spirit of suicide will not operate in my children's lives and influence their behavior. I speak life over my children, and I resist all evil and death.

Father, I thank You for giving my children good friends and mentors. I thank You for blessing them with healthy, safe, and positive social environments and activities.

I believe my children will walk in their God-given purpose, fulfill their assignments in the earth, and make their mark on their generation. God will bless the world through my children, and they will enjoy a life full of happiness, health, prosperity, success, and fulfillment.

I believe they will marry God-loving, spiritually mature spouses, in Jesus' name, amen.

Scripture References

- **Psalm 127:3**

  Lo, children are an heritage of the Lord: and the fruit of the womb is his reward.

- **Proverbs 22:6**

  Train up a child in the way he should go: and when he is old, he will not depart from it.

- **Ephesians 6:4**

  And, ye fathers, provoke not your children to wrath: but bring them up in the nurture and admonition of the Lord.

- **Proverbs 20:11**

  Even a child is known by his doings, whether his work be pure, and whether it be right.

- **Mark 10:14**

  But when Jesus saw it, he was much displeased, and said unto them, Suffer the little children to come unto me, and forbid them not: for of such is the kingdom of God.

- **Luke 17:2**

  It were better for him that a millstone were hanged about his neck, and he cast into the sea, than that he should offend one of these little ones.

- **Proverbs 17:6**

    Children's children are the crown of old men; and the glory of children are their fathers.

- **Proverbs 29:15**

    The rod and reproof give wisdom: but a child left to himself bringeth his mother to shame.

- **Isaiah 54:13**

    And all thy children shall be taught of the Lord; and great shall be the peace of thy children.

- **I Timothy 4:12**

    Let no man despise thy youth; but be thou an example of the believers, in word, in conversation, in charity, in spirit, in faith, in purity.

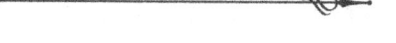

YOUTH

Almost everything that is great has been done by youth.
—Benjamin Disraeli

Our Youth: Teenagers and Young Adults

Father, in the name of Jesus, I lift up our youth before You today—our teenagers and our young adults. I declare that they are taught of the Lord, and great is their peace.

Our youth are whole—spirit, soul, and body. They have healthy self-esteem and know who they are in Christ. Our teenagers and young adults are leaders and never give in to peer pressure. They walk holy and upright before God and man. They are examples of Christ in word and deed and have a consistent, daily quiet time. Our youth grow up into spiritual, personal, and emotional maturity.

They are not rebellious, and show respect for authority at all times. Our teenagers and young adults have quality relationships with their parents, their guardians, and the spiritual authority that You have placed in their lives. They have good Christian fellowship with other believers.

Father, You sent Your Word, healed them, and delivered them from all destruction. Our youth are redeemed from poverty, sickness, failure, and spiritual death. They are redeemed from accidents, terrorism, criminal acts, violence, and street gangs. I plead the Blood of Jesus over them. They are protected from incest, rape, pedophilia, pornography, and all forms of sexual violation.

Our teenagers and young adults are set apart and sanctified unto You. They are not conformed to this world, but they are transformed by the renewing of their minds through the Word of God. They overcome the world, their flesh, and the devil. They have no desire for music filled with ungodly lyrics, premarital sex, adultery, pornography, or any form of perversion. Our youth manage the thoughts of their minds, keep their bodies under control, and stay sexually pure. They have no desire for illicit drugs, smoking, or alcohol.

They resist the devil, and the devil flees from them! They walk out the principles of the Word of God and choose to live for You all the days of their lives.

All of our youth are excellent students. They are the head of their classes and not the tail. They prepare with diligence and use their faith to do well on their schoolwork, tests, and projects. They have favor with their teachers, faculty, and staff. Scholarships, honors, and awards are bestowed upon them.

I declare that our youth fulfill the call, purposes, and plans that You have for their lives, bringing glory and honor to Your name. You have first place in their lives! I declare that they are all tithers and give offerings. There is no lack in their lives—nothing missing, nothing broken, nothing lacking in the lives of our young people.

The angels of the Lord are encamped all around them! The Blood of Jesus covers them, and no weapon formed against them shall prosper. With long life You satisfy them and show them Your salvation!

Now, Holy Spirit, help me to pray fervently and effectually God's perfect will for our teenagers and young adults, in Jesus' name.

Scripture References

- **Proverbs 20:29**

    The glory of young men is their strength: and the beauty of old men is the gray head.

- **Psalm 71:17**

    O God, thou hast taught me from my youth: and hitherto have I declared thy wondrous works.

- **Exodus 20:12**

    Honour thy father and thy mother: that thy days may be long upon the land which the Lord thy God giveth thee.

- **Ephesians 6:2-3**

    ² Honour thy father and mother; (which is the first commandment with promise;) ³ that it may be well with thee, and thou mayest live long on the earth.

- **Proverbs 1:8**

    My son, hear the instruction of thy father, and forsake not the law of thy mother.

- **I Timothy 4:12 (NASB)**

    Let no one look down on your youthfulness, but rather in speech, conduct, love, faith, and purity, show yourself an example of those who believe.

- **Psalm 119:9**

    Wherewithal shall a young man cleanse his way? By taking heed thereto according to thy word.

- **Leviticus 19:32 (NASB)**

    You shall rise up before the grayheaded and honor the aged, and you shall revere your God; I am the Lord.

- **Ezekiel 16:60 (NASB)**

    Nevertheless, I will remember My covenant with you in the days of your youth, and I will establish an everlasting covenant with you.

Challenge in the Conception of a Child

I now release all my fears and concerns about infertility, and I declare myself fertile.

—Unknown

Affirmations for Infertility

1. *I will have a baby in my belly.*
2. *I will never give up hope.*
3. *I have such a positive attitude, and I will get through this tough season.*
4. *I will have the family of my dreams.*

—Carolyn Rich

Challenge in the Conception of a Child

Father, Your Word declares that Your thoughts toward me are thoughts of peace and not of evil, to give me an expected end.

Father, I desire to birth a healthy child of my own with my spouse. You said in Your Word that I would be like a fruitful vine, and my children would be like olive plants around my table. Nothing is too hard for You. I decree it now, in Jesus' name.

I declare and decree that:

1. My womb is blessed.

2. I am loved, I am blessed, and I multiply.

3. I am blessed above all people; therefore, I refuse to be barren in any form.

4. You have taken all sickness and disease away from the midst of me; therefore, no evil will befall me nor any sickness/disease come near me. I thank You that You sent Your Word, You healed me, and You delivered me from all destruction. I sought You, You heard me, and You delivered me from all my fears.

I thank You, Father, for opening my womb like You did for Rebekah, Rachel, and Sarah. I come boldly to the throne of grace to find help in my time of need. I resist all forms of fear! I have thoughts of peace and not of evil because I am inscribed on the palms of Your hands. I know You are ever with me, and Your desire for me is always good.

For this child I pray, and I believe that You have granted me my petition which I asked of You, in Jesus' name.

Conception

Scripture References

- **Philippians 4:6-7**

    ⁶ Be careful for nothing; but in every thing by prayer and supplication with thanksgiving let your requests be made known unto God. ⁷ And the peace of God, which passeth all understanding, shall keep your hearts and minds through Christ Jesus.

- **Jeremiah 29:11**

    For I know the thoughts that I think toward you, saith the Lord, thoughts of peace, and not of evil, to give you an expected end.

- **Psalm 130:5**

    I wait for the Lord, my soul doth wait, and in his word do I hope.

- **Joshua 1:9**

    Have not I commanded thee? Be strong and of good courage; be not afraid, neither be thou dismayed: for the Lord thy God is with thee withersoever thou goest.

- **Genesis 21:2**

    For Sarah conceived, and bare Abraham a son in his old age, at the set time of which God had spoken to him.

- **I Samuel 2:21**

    For the Lord visited Hannah, so that she conceived and bare three sons and two daughters. And the child Samuel grew before the Lord.

Read these verses and declare: Just like the Lord did it for Sarah and Hannah, He will do it for me!

- **Romans 12:12**

    Rejoicing in hope; patient in tribulation; continuing instant in prayer.

- **Psalm 113:9**

    He makes the barren woman to keep house, and to be a joyful mother of children.

- **Psalm 37:5**

    Commit thy way unto the Lord; trust also in Him; and he shall bring it to pass.

- **Genesis 25:21**

    And Isaac intreated the Lord for his wife, because she was barren: and the Lord was intreated of him, and Rebekah his wife conceived.

- **Mark 11:24**

   Therefore I say unto you, What things soever ye desire, when ye pray, believe that ye receive them, and ye shall have them.

- **Psalm 27:14**

   Wait on the Lord: be of good courage, and he shall strengthen thine heart: wait, I say, on the Lord.

- **Deuteronomy 7:14**

   Thou shall be blessed above all people: there shall not be male or female barren among you, or among your cattle.

DECISION-MAKING

*You can't make decisions based on fear
and the possibility of what might happen.*

—*Michelle Obama*

Decision-Making

Father, You said in Your Word that I can approach You with confidence if I ask anything according to Your will. Wisdom for godly direction and decision-making is Your will for my life.

So now, Father, in the name of Jesus, I desire wisdom, direction, and guidance in the area of _____.

Father, guide and direct me in the way that I should go. I put my trust in You, and I lean not to my own understanding. Help me to look at this situation from all angles, and cause me to see things clearly and accurately with Your eye and from Your perspective. Help me to recognize Your part in this matter and also recognize my part and my responsibility. I choose to discipline myself to set aside time in prayer and meditation in Your Word in order to listen for Your guidance. I will not be hasty, impatient, or respond in my flesh. I am Your sheep, and You are my Shepherd. I hear and know Your voice. The voice of a stranger I will not follow. I will follow Your voice and will not base my decision on money, circumstances, feelings, or pressure from people.

Your Word is a lamp unto my feet and a light for my path. Father, You said if I acknowledge You, You would direct my path. I believe You are directing me now, and all of my decisions are consistent with Your will and purpose for my life, in Jesus' name.

Scripture References

- **Proverbs 2:6 (NKJV)**

  For the Lord gives wisdom; From his mouth comes knowledge and understanding.

- **Proverbs 19:2 (NKJV)**

  Also it is not good for a soul to be without knowledge, And he sins who hastens with his feet.

- **Proverbs 16:2 (NKJV)**

  All the ways of a man are pure in his own eyes, but the Lord weighs the spirits.

- **Proverbs 11:14 (NKJV)**

  Where there is no counsel, the people fall; But in the multitude of counselors there is safety.

- **Proverbs 10:17 (NKJV)**

  He who keeps instruction is in the way of life, But he who refuses correction goes astray.

- **Proverbs 16:25 (NKJV)**

  There is a way that seems right to a man, But its end is the way of death.

- **Proverbs 14:1 (NKJV)**

  The wise woman builds her house, But the foolish pulls it down with her hands.

- **Proverbs 10:9 (NKJV)**

  He who walks with integrity walks securely, But he who perverts his ways will become known.

Wisdom

Lessons in life will be repeated until they are learned.

—*Author Unknown*

Intelligence without wisdom brings destruction.

—*Erol Ozan*

Wisdom

Father, Your Word says if any man lacks wisdom, he should ask You for it. I ask You for direction in the area of_____. You also said in all our ways to acknowledge You, and You would direct our path. I acknowledge You in this matter. I recognize that You give wisdom, and out of Your mouth comes knowledge and understanding.

Now, I commit my works upon You. I trust You and roll them wholly upon You. I thank You for causing my thoughts to agree with Your will and establishing my plans for success.

I receive Your wisdom and direction for all the matters of my life. I am no longer wise in my own eyes. I hear the voice of the Good Shepherd, and the voice of a stranger I will not follow. My thoughts are in line with Your thoughts. Father, I now have clear and concise insight on what I need to do. God's Word is a lamp unto my feet and a light unto my path. I always make good decisions and in my pathway is life and not death. God's favor goes before me; it is with me and behind me. I walk in paths that God prepared ahead of time, and I live the good life that God prearranged and made ready for me to live.

Thank You, Father, for guiding me with Your eye. I agree with You that Your thoughts, perspective, and ways are best for me, in Jesus' name.

Scripture References

- **James 1:5**

  If any of you lack wisdom, let him ask of God, that giveth to all men liberally, and upbraideth not; and it shall be given him.

- **James 3:17**

  But the wisdom that is from above is first pure, then peaceable, gentle, and easy to be intreated, full of mercy and good fruits, without partiality, and without hypocrisy.

- **Proverbs 19:20**

  Hear counsel, and receive instruction, that thou mayest be wise in thy latter end.

- **Proverbs 18:15**

  The heart of the prudent getteth knowledge; and the ear of the wise seeketh knowledge.

- **Proverbs 12:15**

  The way of a fool is right in his own eyes: but he that hearkeneth unto counsel is wise.

- **Proverbs 10:23**

  It is as sport to a fool to do mischief: but a man of understanding hath wisdom.

- **Colossians 3:16**

  Let the word of Christ dwell in you richly in all wisdom; teaching and admonishing one another in psalms and hymns and spiritual songs, singing with grace in your hearts to the Lord.

- **Ephesians 5:15-17**

   [15] See then that ye walk circumspectly, not as fools, but as wise, [16] redeeming the time, because the days are evil. [17] Wherefore be ye not unwise, but understanding what the will of the Lord is.

- **Proverbs 2:6**

   For the LORD giveth wisdom: out of his mouth cometh knowledge and understanding.

- **Proverbs 16:16**

   How much better is it to get wisdom than gold! and to get understanding rather to be chosen than silver!

PROSPERITY

Prosperity begins with a state of mind.

—*Anonymous*

Prosperity and Material Success

Father, in Jesus' name, I am blessed and walk not in the counsel of the ungodly, nor stand in the way of sinners, nor sit in the seat of the scornful. I delight in the law of the Lord, and in His law, I meditate day and night.

I am like a tree planted by the rivers of water. I bring forth my fruit in my season. My leaf shall not wither, and whatever I do prospers. I enjoy good success in life.

I am a tither, and I give 10 percent of all my increase to the local church where God has instructed me to connect and serve.

I receive the windows of Heaven's blessings. I receive supernatural ability to function at a high level of excellence and integrity. I receive divine favor, open doors of opportunity, and provision from expected and unexpected means.

In Jesus' name, I declare that satan and demons will not devour or rob me of my return. I am the seed of Abraham and a child of the Most High God. Therefore, I have everything I need to live a first-class lifestyle.

I am a giver, and I follow Jesus' lifestyle of giving. I give and it is given unto me good measure, pressed down, shaken together, and running over. I am not afraid. I start with what I have, and God gives me more. I resist pride, and I am a good receiver. The Lord is my shepherd, and I do not experience lack, scarcity, or unfulfilled desires. I have more than enough to take vacations and enjoy time with my family. I believe all my needs are met, my bills are paid in a timely manner, and I am totally free from debt. The blessing of the Lord is on my life, and I experience no sorrow.

I have all the finances I need to (1) give to God; (2) give to others/ministries; and (3) give for the education of my children and others. My giving to the poor is a loan to the Lord, and He is faithful to pay me back. Because I give to the poor, there is no lack in my life. God continues to give me more so that I can continue to be a blessing to those who lack. God's grace abounds toward me, and I always have an abundance for my personal life and an abundance to bless others. I am a kingdom investor and a kingdom philanthropist.

I am a wise money manager and a good steward over the resources God gives me. God is my source, so I look to him for wisdom and direction. I hear his voice and the voice of satan, demons, the world, and my flesh, I will not follow. I am not wasteful, impatient, impulsive, or gullible. I am a wise money manager.

I take a lesson from the ants. I am not lazy, but wise. I work smart, plan well, and have savings. I only invest in successful, godly, profit-producing endeavors. I prepare for the future and my descendants by having a will/trust and insurance. I leave them a wealthy inheritance, in Jesus' name.

Scripture References

- **Deuteronomy 8:18**

  But thou shalt remember the LORD thy God: for it is he that giveth thee power to get wealth, that he may establish his covenant which he sware unto thy fathers, as it is this day.

- **Jeremiah 29:11**

  For I know the thoughts that I think toward you, saith the LORD, thoughts of peace, and not of evil, to give you an expected end.

- **Philippians 4:19**

  But my God shall supply all your need according to his riches in glory by Christ Jesus.

- **Malachi 3:10**

  Bring ye all the tithes into the storehouse, that there may be meat in mine house, and prove me now herewith, saith the LORD of hosts, if I will not open you the windows of heaven, and pour you out a blessing, that there shall not be room enough to receive it.

- **III John 1:2**

  Beloved, I wish above all things that thou mayest prosper and be in health, even as thy soul prospereth.

- **Joshua 1:8**

  This book of the law shall not depart out of thy mouth; but thou shalt meditate therein day and night, that thou mayest observe to do according to all that is written therein: for then thou shalt make thy way prosperous, and then thou shalt have good success.

- **II Corinthians 9:8**

  And God is able to make all grace abound toward you; that ye, always having all sufficiency in all things, may abound to every good work:

- **Joshua 1:9**

  Have not I commanded thee? Be strong and of a good courage; be not afraid, neither be thou dismayed: for the Lord by God is with thee withersoever thou goest.

- **Psalm 1:3**

  And he shall be like a tree planted by the rivers of water, that bringeth forth his fruit in his season; his leaf also shall not wither; and whatsoever he doeth shall prosper.

- **II Corinthians 8:9**

  For ye know the grace of our Lord Jesus Christ, that, though he was rich, yet for your sakes he became poor, that ye through his poverty might be rich.

- **Luke 6:38**

  Give, and it shall be given unto you; good measure, pressed down, and shaken together, and running over, shall men give into your bosom. For with the same measure that ye mete withal it shall be measured to you again.

CHRISTIAN BUSINESS OWNER

*Don't be afraid to go out on a limb.
That's where the fruit is.*

—H. Jackson Brown, Jr.

Christian Business Owner

Father, I declare that Jesus is Lord of my life, and You are the head of my business. My business is built on sound business principles and governed by a biblical blueprint. I thank You for giving me a clear vision, an excellent plan, organizational structure, and successful strategies.

My business is committed to offering quality products and services that are customer focused. We are diligent and organized to meet our customers' needs in an excellent and timely fashion. Integrity is important to us, and keeping our word is our commitment to our customers. We appreciate feedback and view complaints as a gift to make us better.

We hire the best people for the job who have both great technical and people skills. All of our employees and volunteers are honest, kind, compassionate, and hardworking. Our staff exhibits great teamwork and quickly and effectively work through and resolve conflict issues. We are all open to learn from our mistakes, and take responsibility for growing and becoming better at what we do.

My business is creative, innovative, and always relevant in regard to the needs of customers and changes in the culture and business environment.

My business is highly profitable, creating wealth and influence. Through the success of my business, I can provide a high quality of life for my family, generously invest in the Kingdom of God, expand the business, and grow.

Thank You, Father, for blessing the works of my hands.

Your blessing has made my business rich, and there is no sorrow, in Jesus' name.

Christian Business Owner Confessions

1. I believe in my product/service and myself. God supplies all my needs for my business: money, buildings, good employees, favor, etc. I am a forward-thinking business owner.

2. Those times when no one believes in my business, vision, and dreams, I won't be afraid because God said don't be afraid, just believe. I have the money to pay my workers a good salary and pay them in a timely manner. I have a topnotch business team. I am a good boss, mentor, and friend to others in business. The favor of God operates in my life daily.

3. When I have to make a difficult decision or have a difficult meeting, I always acknowledge God for wisdom. I am not easily offended, and I am quick to forgive. I am mentally strong.

4. I have work balance, and I prioritize my life. I have time for family, customers, friends, and recreation. I get plenty of rest, exercise, and I have a healthy diet.

5. I am increasing in knowledge in my business. I am a lifelong learner. I have a growth plan, and I am a student of business. I learn from all of my mistakes.

6. I have a business plan so that I can analyze each business transaction, research, and compile data to make conclusions based on facts from my research.

7. My business is redeemed from: (1) theft, (2) lack, (3) inflation, (4) recession, (5) drought, and (6) natural disasters.

a. No weapon formed against my business shall prosper. A thousand may fall at my side and ten thousand at my right hand, but no evil will come nigh my business.

8. God gives me creative ideas to generate money for my business. The Lord will command blessings in my business and all that my hands touch. I am a wise money manager and a wise manager of my time and energy.

9. Because I have the fruit of the Spirit operating in my life, my services are customer-friendly. I treat customers fairly, and I will always remain grateful for my customers.

10. I strive to be a master in the art of negotiation.

11. I believe I have a great retirement plan.

Scripture References

- **Exodus 35:35**

  Them hath he filled with wisdom of heart, to work all manner of work, of the engraver, and of the cunning workman, and of the embroiderer, in blue, and in purple, in scarlet, and in fine linen, and of the weaver, even of them that do any work, and of those that devise cunning work.

- **Nehemiah 6:9**

  For they all made us afraid, saying, Their hands shall be weakened from the work, that it be not done. Now therefore, O God, strengthen my hands.

- **Psalm 112:5**

  A good man sheweth favour, and lendeth: he will guide his affairs with discretion.

- **Proverbs 10:4**

  He becometh poor that dealeth with a slack hand; but the hand of the diligent maketh rich.

- **Proverbs 13:4**

  The soul of the sluggard desireth, and hath nothing: but the soul of the diligent shall be made fat.

- **Proverbs 13:11**

  Wealth gotten by vanity shall be diminished: but he that gathereth by labour shall increase.

- **Proverbs 16:8**

  Better is a little with righteousness than great revenues without right.

- **Proverbs 21:5**

  The thoughts of the diligent tend only to plenteousness; but every one that is hasty only to want.

- **Luke 16:10**

  He that is faithful in that which is least is faithful also in much: and he that is unjust in the least is unjust also in much.

- **Colossians 3:23**

  And whatsoever ye do, do it heartily, as to the Lord, and not unto men.

CAREER

*If you can't figure out your purpose,
figure out your passion. For passion will lead you
right into purpose.*

—*T.D. Jakes*

Career Decisions

Father God, I pray that You would guide/direct me as I search for a career in life. I want to walk out the plan and purpose You have for my life. I pray for supernatural wisdom, favor, determination, confidence, and courage.

Help me find and believe in the gifts and talents that You have bestowed on me when I was in my mother's womb. I pray that I walk/grow in these gifts and talents all of my days.

Give me favor as I go on interviews. I pray that the interviews will go well and that I stand out above the crowd.

Help me not to be distracted by what my friends are doing or not doing. Help me to keep my eyes focused on my purpose in life and not on others. Help me not to compare myself with others.

Thank You in advance for ordering my steps and leading me to a fulfilling and meaningful career, in Jesus' name.

Scripture References

- **Ecclesiastes 9:10**

    Whatsoever thy hand findeth to do, do it with thy might; for there is no work, nor device, nor knowledge, nor wisdom, in the grave, whither thou goest.

- **Matthew 6:34**

    Take therefore no thought for the morrow: for the morrow shall take thought for the things of itself. Sufficient unto the day is the evil thereof.

- **Proverbs 20:18**

    Every purpose is established by counsel: and with good advice make war.

- **Proverbs 3:5-6**

    ⁵Trust in the Lord with all thine heart; and lean not unto thine own understanding. ⁶In all thy ways acknowledge him, and he shall direct thy paths.

- **Psalm 32:8**

    I will instruct thee and teach thee in the way which thou shall go: I will guide thee with mine eye.

- **Proverbs 19:21**

    There are many devices in a man's heart; nevertheless the counsel of the Lord, that shall stand.

- **Psalm 37:4**

    Delight thyself also in the Lord; and he shall give thee the desires of thine heart.

- **Jeremiah 17:7**

    Blessed is the man that trusteth in the Lord, and whose hope the Lord is.

Healing

*The moment you change your perception,
is the moment you rewrite the chemistry in your body.*

—Dr. Bruce Lipton

Healing, Health, and Long Life

Father, in Jesus' name, I thank You that Jesus took my infirmities, bore my sicknesses, and by His stripes, I was healed.

The Holy Spirit lives in me, and He is quickening my mortal flesh. He is causing the life of Jesus to be made manifest in my body. I walk in divine health, and I am satisfied with a long, healthy life.

The words that I speak over my body today are life and health.

All 206 bones in my body have all the minerals/vitamins they need to be strong and healthy. My bones are free from arthritis, osteoporosis, breakage, cancer, tumors, and all forms of sickness and disease.

All the systems of my body—circulatory, cardiovascular, endocrine, integumentary, exocrine, lymphatic, immune, muscular, skeletal, renal, urinary, and every other system—function the way God created them to function, free of sickness and disease.

I am the temple of the Holy Spirit; therefore, sickness, disease, viruses, infections, and inflammation cannot coexist, dominate, or remain in my body.

I believe the reports from my physician agree with the Word of God. All my test results come back negative.

I believe I exercise on a regular basis; therefore, my mood is improved, and my energy is boosted. I sleep better, and my weight is under better control. I drink the proper amount of water daily to rid my body of toxins and keep me hydrated. I have a healthy diet. I watch the portion size of my meals and my salt and sugar intake. My blood pressure is 120/80. My cholesterol levels are at a perfect balance. My mind is alert, and my memory is blessed. I am free from all diseases/conditions of the mind: depression, mental illness, tumors, masses, seizures, concussions, inflammation, abscesses, meningitis, and Alzheimer's. I don't hold grudges, and I am quick to forgive. I am worry-free because I cast all my cares/concerns over to the Lord. I thank You that my broken heart is healed. I will not allow stress/anxiety to rob me of energy, vitality, and shorten my life.

My youth is renewed like the eagles. I live a strong, healthy, and long life. I will finish my course and my God-given purpose in life. Then, I will come to my grave in a full age with no sickness, disease, dementia, mental loss, or need for aid or support. I will just fall asleep in Jesus and wake up in Heaven, in Jesus' name.

Scripture References

- **Psalm 107:20**

  He sent his word, and healed them, and delivered them from their destructions.

- **Deuteronomy 34:7**

  And Moses was an hundred and twenty years old when he died: his eye was not dim, nor his natural force abated.

- **Mark 11:23**

  For verily I say unto you, That whosoever shall say unto this mountain, Be thou removed, and be thou cast into the sea; and shall not doubt in his heart, but shall believe that those things which he saith shall come to pass; he shall have whatsoever he saith.

- **I Peter 2:24**

  Who his own self bare our sins in his own body on the tree, that we, being dead to sins, should live unto righteousness: by whose stripes ye were healed.

- **Psalm 118:17**

  I shall not die, but live, and declare the works of the Lord.

- **Psalm 91:16**

  With long life will I satisfy him, and shew him my salvation.

- **John 10:10b**

  I am come that they might have life, and that they might have it more abundantly.

- **III John 1:2**

  Beloved, I wish above all things that thou mayest prosper and be in health, even as thy soul prospereth.

- **James 5:15**

  And the prayer of faith shall save the sick, and the Lord shall raise him up; and if he have committed sins, they shall be forgiven him.

- **Jeremiah 17:14**

    Heal me, Oh Lord, and I shall be healed; save me, and I shall be saved: for thou art my praise.

- **II Kings 20:5b**

    I have heard thy prayer, I have seen thy tears: behold, I will heal thee:

First Holiday Without a Loved One

God gave us the gift of memory!
—*Minister Connie Blaylock*

First Holiday Without a Loved One

Father God, I come to You in Jesus' name, and I thank You for being the Father of Mercies and the God of All Comfort. Your Word says that You are a very present help in trouble. Therefore, I confess that You are my refuge and strength.

Because You are with me and in me, I choose to not allow my heart to be troubled, neither will I allow it to be afraid. Your Holy Spirit is abiding in me, and I am yielding to Him. He is my Comforter, Guide, Intercessor, Strengthener, Helper, Counselor, and Standby. I am not alone. He is greater than death, grief, sorrow, and loneliness.

You said in Your Word that You left us with your peace—a peace that passes all understanding. I receive this wonderful gift.

This entire holiday season, I choose peace and joy. I resist grief, sadness, regret, guilt, and everything that will attempt to destroy me or hinder me from enjoying this wonderful time of the year. I will focus on others, your goodness, and my blessings. I will not focus on my loss or on myself, in Jesus' name.

Scripture References

- **I Thessalonians 4:13-14**

    [13] But I would not have you to be ignorant, brethren, concerning them which are asleep, that ye sorrow not,

even as others which have no hope. ¹⁴ For if we believe that Jesus died and rose again, even so them also which sleep in Jesus will God bring with him.

- **John 11:25-26 (NIV)**

  ²⁵ Jesus said to her, "I am the resurrection and the life. The one who believes in me will live, even though they die; ²⁶ and whoever lives by believing in me will never die. Do you believe this?"

- **II Corinthians 5:8**

  We are confident, I say, and willing rather to be absent from the body, and to be present with the Lord.

- **John 14:1-2**

  ¹ Let not your heart be troubled: ye believe in God, believe also in me. ² In my Father's house are many mansions: if it were not so, I would have told you. I go to prepare a place for you.

- **Revelation 21:4 (NIV)**

  He will wipe every tear from their eyes. There will be no more death or mourning or crying or pain, for the old order of things has passed away.

- **I Thessalonians 4:17-18 (NIV)**

  ¹⁷ After that, we who are still alive and are left will be caught up together with them in the clouds to meet the Lord in the air. And so we will be with the Lord forever. ¹⁸ Therefore encourage one another with these words.

- **Psalm 48:14 (NIV)**

  For this God is our God for ever and ever; he will be our guide even to the end.

- **Philippians 2:20 (NIV)**

  I have no one else like him, who will show genuine concern for your welfare.

PROTECTION

*You are safe not because of the absence of danger,
but because of the presence of God.*

—Author Unknown

*If God be with us, we have no cause for fear.
His eye is upon us, his arm over us, his ear open
to our prayer, his grace sufficient,
his promise unchangeable.*

—John Newton

Protection

Father, today I confess Psalm 91 over my life. I say, I dwell in the secret place of the Most High, and I abide under the shadow of the Almighty.

Lord, I say You are my refuge and my fortress, and in You, I will trust. I thank You for delivering me from the snare of the fowler and from the noisome pestilence. I will not be captured by any trap satan sets. I am protected from every epidemic that comes upon the earth.

Lord, You cover me with Your feathers, and under Your wings, I trust. Your Word is my shield and buckler. I am not afraid of the terror by night, nor the arrow that flies by day, nor for the pestilence that walks in darkness, nor for destruction at noonday. I am redeemed and protected from all forms of accidents and injuries. Satan shall not steal from me through unlawful home invasions, car jackings, identity theft, or any form of thievery. I am protected from all criminal activity, terrorism, violence, and evil works. Rape, incest, pedophilia, and every form of sexual assault and violation shall not come near me and my family. I am redeemed from adverse weather conditions: hurricanes, tornadoes, earthquakes, fires, flooding, thunderstorms, and drought.

A thousand shall fall at my side and ten thousand at my right hand, but it won't come near me.

I choose the Lord as my refuge. The Most High is my habitation; therefore, no evil shall happen to me and no sickness or disease shall come near me or my household. The angels of

God have been given charge over me, and they keep me in all my ways. They bear me up in their hands, and I do not fall. I walk on serpents and scorpions, and nothing shall by any means hurt me. I have set my love on the Lord, and He delivers me and sets me on high. In times of trouble, He delivers me when I call on His name. All things, satan, demons, and evil are under my feet. I honor the Lord my God, and He satisfies me with a long, strong, and healthy life.

In Jesus' name, I overcome satan by the Blood of Jesus and the word of my testimony. According to Jesus, the head of the Church, I have what I say and experience it now, in Jesus' name.

Scripture References

Psalm 91

[1] He that dwelleth in the secret place of the most High shall abide under the shadow of the Almighty.

[2] I will say of the LORD, He is my refuge and my fortress: my God; in him will I trust.

[3] Surely he shall deliver thee from the snare of the fowler, and from the noisome pestilence.

[4] He shall cover thee with his feathers, and under his wings shalt thou trust: his truth shall be thy shield and buckler.

[5] Thou shalt not be afraid for the terror by night; nor for the arrow that flieth by day;

⁶ Nor for the pestilence that walketh in darkness; nor for the destruction that wasteth at noonday.

⁷ A thousand shall fall at thy side, and ten thousand at thy right hand; but it shall not come nigh thee.

⁸ Only with thine eyes shalt thou behold and see the reward of the wicked.

⁹ Because thou hast made the LORD, which is my refuge, even the most High, thy habitation;

¹⁰ There shall no evil befall thee, neither shall any plague come nigh thy dwelling.

¹¹ For he shall give his angels charge over thee, to keep thee in all thy ways.

¹² They shall bear thee up in their hands, lest thou dash thy foot against a stone.

¹³ Thou shalt tread upon the lion and adder: the young lion and the dragon shalt thou trample under feet.

¹⁴ Because he hath set his love upon me, therefore will I deliver him: I will set him on high, because he hath known my name.

¹⁵ He shall call upon me, and I will answer him: I will be with him in trouble; I will deliver him, and honour him.

¹⁶ With long life will I satisfy him, and shew him my salvation.

FEAR

I learned that courage was not the absence of fear, but the triumph over it. The brave man is not he who does not feel afraid, but he who conquers that fear.

—Nelson Mandela

Fear

Father, I commit myself to walk in faith and not in fear. I realize that fear opens the door to satan to steal, kill, and destroy. I resist fear because fear will derail and sabotage Your plan for my life. Now that You have delivered me out of the hand of the enemy, I choose to serve You without fear. When I am tempted to be afraid, I am reminded of Your Word. You said You would never leave me and that You would always be with me to protect me from all hurt, harm, or danger.

I trust You for being my loving Father and always having my best interest at heart.

Your Word declares that You have not given me the spirit of fear, so I claim power, love, and a sound mind.

I am seeking You today, and You have delivered me from all my fears.

- I will not fear man.
- I will not fear commitment.
- I will not fear shortage or lack.
- I will not fear decision-making.
- I will not fear change.
- I will not fear rejection.
- I will not fear the future.
- I will not fear failure.

- I will not fear inadequacy.
- I will not fear sickness.
- I will not fear death.

I realize that I am not totally responsible for caring for myself or handling the situations in my life. I trust You to be my wisdom, strength, ability, and support.

I break the power of fear and its attempt to control and dominate my life. I resist fear! I focus on Your Word and exercise courage by facing fear. I choose to do what I am tempted to be afraid of. I don't draw back, but I push forward, in Jesus' name.

Scripture References

- **II Timothy 1:7**

    For God hath not given us the spirit of fear; but of power, and of love, and of a sound mind.

- **I Peter 5:7**

    Casting all your care upon him; for he careth for you.

- **Isaiah 41:10**

    Fear thou not; for I am with the: be not dismayed; for I am thy God: I will strengthen thee; yes, I will help thee; yea, I will uphold thee with the right hand of my righteousness.

- **John 16:33**

  These things I have spoken unto you, that in me ye might have peace. In the world ye shall have tribulation: but be of good cheer, I have overcome the world.

- **Romans 8:38-39 (NKJV)**

  ³⁸ For I am persuaded that neither death nor life, nor angels nor principalities nor powers, nor things present nor things to come, ³⁹ nor height nor depth, nor any other created thing, shall be able to separate us from the love of God which is in Christ Jesus our Lord.

- **Romans 8:15**

  For ye have not received the spirit of bondage again to fear; but ye have received the Spirit of adoption, whereby we cry, Abba, Father.

- **Proverbs 1:7**

  The fear of the Lord is the beginning of knowledge: but fools despise wisdom and instruction.

- **Psalm 27:1**

  The Lord is my light and my salvation; whom shall I fear? the Lord is the strength of my life; of whom shall I be afraid?

FAVOR

Favor opens any door while it remains closed for everyone else.

—Sunday Adelaja

Favor

Father, I thank You for Your favor being on my life. I am increasing in wisdom and stature and favor with You and men. Your favor is manifested in all my relationships and all my activities. I walk in undeserved and unmerited blessings on a daily basis. It is not by my power or the might of my hand that I enjoy success, prosperity, and wealth. Father, You are the source of my blessings, and it is You that gives me the power to get wealth.

Because of Your anointing grace and strength, I operate at a high level of excellence and integrity in all that I do. You are blessing the works of my hand. I thank You for raising up people who are willing to use their position and resources to help me to achieve my goals and fulfill the dreams You put in my heart. Because of Your favor in and on my life, I am recognized, preferred, accepted, and promoted. I thank You for giving me confidence in my God-given abilities, and I don't fear rejection or failure. I expect to succeed in all I do. I believe You are ordering my steps, and in my pathway are prearranged resources set aside for my well-being.

Thank You for preferential treatment in all my affairs. As I abound in Your favor, I freely dispense Your favor to others, in Jesus' name.

Scripture References

- **Genesis 39:21**

    But the LORD was with Joseph, and shewed him mercy, and gave him favour in the sight of the keeper of the prison.

- **I Samuel 2:26**

    And the child Samuel grew on, and was in favour both with the LORD, and also with men.

- **Proverbs 3:4**

    So shalt thou find favour and good understanding in the sight of God and man.

- **Proverbs 8:35**

    For whoso findeth me findeth life, and shall obtain favour of the Lord.

- **Proverbs 12:2**

    A good man obtaineth favour of the Lord: but a man of wicked devices will he condemn.

- **Numbers 6:25**

    The Lord make his face shine upon thee, and be gracious unto thee.

- **Psalm 119:135**

    Make thy face to shine upon thy servant; and teach me thy statutes.

- **Jeremiah 32:41**

    Yea, I will rejoice over them to do them good, and I will plant them in this land assuredly with my whole heart and with my whole soul.

- **Psalm 80:3**

    Turn us again, O God, and cause thy face to shine; and we shall be saved.

- **I John 3:22**

    And whatsoever we ask, we receive of him, because we keep his commandments, and do those things that are pleasing in his sight.

LOW SELF-ESTEEM

*Too many people overvalue what they are not
and undervalue what they are.*

—*Malcolm S. Forbes*

Prayer for Low Self-Esteem

Father God, I have allowed my circumstances and experiences in life, whether through parents, authority figures, race, friends, etc., to tell me who I am in life and not Your Word. Help me to see who I am and what I am capable of doing through Your Word and not the situations and circumstances of my life.

Help me not to see my worth through my relationships. I choose to see myself through the eyes of these Scriptures:

1. Jesus died on the cross for me so that I could have eternal life (John 3:16). How could I say I am not worthy or needed?

2. I am of more value than many sparrows (Luke 12:7; Matthew 10:31).

3. I am the workmanship of a perfect God (Ephesians 2:10).

4. I am flawless in God's eyes (Song of Solomon 4:7).

5. I am created in the image of God (Genesis 1:26-27).

6. I am fearfully and wonderfully made (Psalm 139:14).

7. I am His beloved (1 John 3:1-2).

8. I am forgiven (Hebrews 8:12).

9. I am His treasured possession (Deuteronomy 26:18).

10. His mercy for me endures forever (I Chronicles 16:34).

11. I am loved dearly (Colossians 3:12).

12. He will never leave or forsake me (Deuteronomy 31:6).

13. I am blessed by His hands (Psalm 139:5).

14. I am a good and perfect gift (James 1:17).

15. I am valuable to God (Luke 12:7).

16. I am the work of His hands (Isaiah 64:8).

I believe what Your Word says about me, in Jesus' name, amen.

Scripture References

- **Philippians 4:13**

    I can do all things through Christ which strengtheneth me.

- **Psalm 46:5**

    God is in the midst of her; she shall not be moved: God shall help her, and that right early.

- **Isaiah 43:4**

    Since thou wast precious in my sight, thou hast been honourable, and I have loved thee: therefore will I give men for thee, and people for thy life.

- **Luke 12:7**

  But even the very hairs of your head are all numbered. Fear not therefore: ye are of more value than many sparrows.

- **Ephesians 2:10**

  For we are his workmanship, created in Christ Jesus unto good works, which God hath before ordained that we should walk in them.

- **Psalm 139:14**

  I will praise thee; for I am fearfully and wonderfully made: marvelous are thy works; and that my soul knoweth right well.

- **Matthew 10:31**

  Fear ye not therefore, ye are of more value than many sparrows.

- **Jeremiah 31:3**

  The Lord hath appeared of old unto me, saying, Yea, I have loved thee with an everlasting love: therefore with lovingkindness have I drawn thee.

- **I John 4:4**

  Ye are of God, little children, and have overcome them: because greater is he that is in you, than he that is in the world.

- **Galatians 4:7**

  Wherefore thou art no more a servant, but a son; and if a son, then an heir of God through Christ.

20 Positive Affirmations[2]

1. I am worthy of love and happiness.
2. I am in alignment with my soul purpose.
3. I allow new beginnings in my life.
4. I choose to see the bright side.
5. I am unaffected by the judgement of others.
6. I am grateful for all that I have.
7. I don't fail, I learn.
8. Every obstacle is an opportunity to grow.
9. Today and everyday, I choose to be happy.
10. I make peace with what I can't control.
11. I am a magnet for positivity and blessings.
12. I forgive myself.
13. I am determined to succeed.
14. I am resilient.
15. I release all my doubt and insecurities about myself.
16. I am allowed to say yes to myself and no to others.

---

[2] Positive Affirmations taken from ellduclos.blog.

17. I am talented and intelligent.

18. I trust my intuition, and I always make wise decisions.

19. I am stronger than my excuses.

20. I am a winner.

My thoughts for today

Date: _____

_____
_____
_____
_____
_____
_____
_____
_____
_____
_____
_____

*Commit thy works unto the Lord,
and thy thoughts shall be established.
(Proverbs 16:3)*

My thoughts for today

Date: _____

_____
_____
_____
_____
_____
_____
_____
_____
_____
_____

*Every way of a man is right in his own eyes:
but the LORD pondereth the hearts.
(Proverbs 21:2)*

My thoughts for today

Date: _____

_____
_____
_____
_____
_____
_____
_____
_____
_____
_____
_____
_____

For my thoughts are not your thoughts,
neither are your ways my ways, saith the Lord.
(Isaiah 55:8)

My thoughts for today

Date: _____

_____
_____
_____
_____
_____
_____
_____
_____
_____
_____
_____

[1] O Lord, thou hast searched me, and known me.
[2] Thou knowest my downsitting and mine uprising, thou understandest my thought afar off.
(Psalm 139:1-2)

My thoughts for today

Date: _____

*For I know the thoughts that I have toward you,
said the Lord, thoughts of peace, and not of evil,
to give you an expected end.
(Jeremiah 29:11)*

My thoughts for today

Date: _____

_____
_____
_____
_____
_____
_____
_____
_____
_____
_____

*Ponder the path of thy feet,
and let all thy ways be established.
(Proverbs 4:26)*

About the Author

Kennetha J. Moore was born and raised in Lynch, Kentucky. She graduated from Berea College in Berea, Kentucky. She has been in ministry at Faith Chapel along with her husband, Mike Moore, for 41 years. Through faith in God's Word, they have a thriving ministry in Birmingham, Alabama and Columbus, Georgia. Kennetha is a Bible teacher, a certified teacher of leadership from John Maxwell's Leadership Program, a camp director, an intercessor, and an impactful leader in various other roles throughout her time in ministry. Her greatest role is that of being a wife, a mother of two, and a grandmother to three beautiful girls.

About Mike Moore Ministries

Mike Moore Ministries, a global ministry founded by Mike Moore, was built upon the simple yet profound truth that "The Word of God is the Answer" to all of life's questions. Through various mediums which include television, digital, and print, Moore teaches that God wants His people to live a prosperous life— a prosperity that exceeds the boundaries of just finances. This prosperity encompasses spiritual prosperity, physical health, relationships, mental health, and financial independence.

MIKE MOORE
MINISTRIES

Additional resources can be obtained by visiting **mikemoore.com** or by calling toll-free
1-866-930-WORD (9673).

Weep Not

Overcoming Grief, Disappointment, and Loss

MIKE MOORE

At some point, everyone will experience the death of a loved one. To most people, death is a heart-rending, mind-boggling, terrifying experience. However, according to the Bible, we should not be fearful or sorrowful at the departure of a loved one because physical death is not the end of life. In this illuminating book, *Weep Not - Overcoming Grief, Disappointment and Loss*, Moore exposes the subtle way that Satan uses the death of a loved one to cause guilt, sorrow, depression and hopelessness. Your life is not over just because your relationship is over. When you discover how to overcome grief, disappointment and loss, you will realize that the best is yet to come!

ORDER TODAY!

at www.mikemoore.com
ISBN: 978-0-8814431-1-0

Healing Is for All
Mike Moore

Is divine healing for everybody in the body of Christ? Is it God's will for all His children to be healthy and free from sickness? Is it God's will to heal only some and leave others sick or in pain for His glory or to develop their character? The greatest barrier to the faith of many seeking healing is the uncertainty in our minds as to whether it is the will of God to heal all. Nearly everyone knows that God is able to heal and that He does heal some, but there is much in modern beliefs that keep people from knowing what the Bible really teaches – that *Healing Is for All*. Healing and health are available to you right now!

ISBN: 978-1-7333716-0-5
4"x6" paperback
ORDER TODAY at mikemoore.com

Made in the USA
Middletown, DE
19 September 2025